Getting Around

How We Get Around

Rebecca Rissman

Heinemann LIBRARY

www.heinemannlibrary.co.uk
Visit our website to find out more information about Heinemann Library books.

To order:
☎ Phone +44 (0) 1865 888066
🖷 Fax +44 (0) 1865 314091
🖳 Visit www.heinemannlibrary.co.uk

Heinemann Library is an imprint of Capstone Global Library Limited, a company incorporated in England and Wales having its registered office at 7 Pilgrim Street, London, EC4V 6LB – Registered company number: 6695582

"Heinemann" is a registered trademark of Pearson Education Limited, under licence to Capstone Global Library Limited

Text © Capstone Global Library Limited 2009
First published in hardback in 2009
The moral rights of the proprietor have been asserted.

Edited by Rebecca Rissman, Siân Smith, and Charlotte Guillain
Designed by Kimberly Miracle and Joanna Malivoire
Picture research by Tracy Cummins and Kim Tidwell
Originated by Heinemann Library
Printed in China by Leo Paper Group

ISBN 978 0 431194 18 9
13 12 11 10 09
10 9 8 7 6 5 4 3 2 1

British Library Cataloguing in Publication Data

Rissman, Rebecca

How we get around. - (Acorn plus)

1. Transportation - Pictorial works - Juvenile literature

I. Title

388

Acknowledgments

The author and publishers are grateful to the following for permission to reproduce copyright material: Getty Images pp.**6 left** (©Glow Images), **7 bottom left** (©Riser/PM Images), **10** (©Blend Images/Jeremy Woodhouse), **12** (©Digital Vision), **16** (©Collection Mix: Subjects/Check Six), **18** (©Gallo Images/Christopher Allan); Jupiterimages pp.**8** (©Robert Harding/Bruno Barbier), **14** (©Thinkstock Images), **20** (©Robert Harding/Amanda Hall), **21** (©Smart Creatives/Corbis Images); Shutterstock pp.**6 right** (©egd), **7 bottom left** (©arway), **7 top left** (©Can Balcioglu), **7 top right** (©Taolmor), **9 left** (©Steven Pepple), **9 right** (©Gorilla), **11 left** (©Michael Mattox), **11 middle** (©Peter Weber), **11 right** (©Cheryl Casey), **13 left** (©zeber), **13 right** (©Arphotography), **15 left** (©Ulrich Willmünder), **15 right** (©Tan Wei Ming), **17** (©Ramon Berk), **19 left** (©Javarman), **19 right** (©Ben Smith), **22** (©Razumovskaya Marina Nikolaevna); SuperStock pp.**4** (©Big Cheese Photo), **5** (©age fotostock).

Front cover photograph reproduced with permission of Getty Images (©David Sanger). Back cover photograph reproduced with permission of Shutterstock ©TAOLMOR

We would like to thank Nancy Harris and Adriana Scalise for their help in the preparation of this book.

Every effort has been made to contact copyright holders of any material reproduced in this book. Any omissions will be rectified in subsequent printings if notice is given to the publisher.

Contents

Some words are shown in bold, **like this**. They are explained in "Words to know" on page 23.

Getting around

Every day people move from place to place.

We **travel** from place to place.

Some places are close together. Some places are
far apart.

There are many ways to get from place to place.

On foot

Sometimes people go from place to place by foot.
Some people go by foot because they have no **transport**.
Some people go by foot because they want exercise.

People can walk from place to place. People can run from place to place.

By bicycle

wheels

Sometimes people ride bicycles from place to place.
Bicycles move on **wheels**.

People ride different types of cycles. **Unicycles** have one wheel. Bicycles have two wheels. **Tricycles** have three wheels.

By car

wheels

Sometimes people drive in cars from place to place.
Cars move on **wheels**.

Cars use **engines** to move. Some cars move very fast.
Some cars move slowly.

By train

tracks

Sometimes people **travel** in trains from place to place. Trains move on **tracks**.

Some trains travel above the ground. Some trains travel **underground**.

By plane

Sometimes people fly in planes from place to place.
Planes fly in the air.

wing

engine

Planes have **engines** to help them fly. Planes use **wings** to fly.

By boat

Sometimes people **travel** in boats from place to place. Boats **float** on water.

engine

oar

Some boats use **engines** to get from place to place.
Some boats are **rowed** by people.

Why people move

People move from place to place for many reasons. People **travel** to go to work. People travel to go to school.

People travel to see new places. People travel for fun.

Why do you move?

Why do you move from place to place?

Words to know

engine — machine that uses power to help something move. Cars and planes use engines to move.

float — to stay on top of a liquid. Boats float on water.

oar — a long pole used to push a boat across water

row — to push a boat across water using oars

track — metal rails that guide a train

transport — vehicles that you travel in. Cars, boats, and planes are all types of transport.

travel — to move from place to place

tricycle — cycle with three wheels

underground — below the ground

unicycle — cycle with one wheel

vehicle — something that carries people or things. For example a lorry or a plane

wheel — an object shaped like a circle that turns. Cars and bikes use wheels to move.

wing — long, flat part of a plane that helps it to fly

Index

Notes for parents and teachers

Before reading

Discuss with children that people all around the world move from place to place in different ways. Explain that if places are close together then people can walk, run, or ride a bicycle to move from place to place. If places are far apart then people might travel by car, by bus, by train, by boat, or by plane. Ask children why people need to move from place to place.

After reading

- Make a class graph entitled "Ways we travel to school." Begin by discussing the ways they travel to school (bus, walk, car, bike). Create a pictogram together that shows the ways children get to school. Discuss the graph by asking the following questions: Which way of getting to school do the most (or biggest number of) children use? Which way of getting to school do the least (or smallest number of) children use? Why do you think our graph came out this way?

- Children can create an illustrated book showing the different ways people move from place to place. Headings could include: Wheels, Engines, On a track, and so on.

- Take the children outside. Ask them to walk, crawl, skip, jump, and run. Ask them which way of moving was the fastest and which was the slowest. Encourage children to think of the different ways people get from place to place. Ask them to think of the fastest type of transportation that people use. Get them to act out that type of transportation and then to share what they chose and why.